AS IF LIGHT ACTUALLY MATTERS

NEW & SELECTED POEMS

Books and Chapbooks by Larry D. Thomas

Books

2001: *Amazing Grace* (poems), Texas Review Press, Huntsville, Texas
2004: *Where Skulls Speak Wind* (poems), Texas Review Press, Huntsville, Texas
2005: *Stark Beauty* (poems), Timberline Press, Fulton, Missouri
2008: *The Fraternity of Oblivion* (poems), Timberline Press, Fulton, Missouri
2008: *Larry D. Thomas: TCU Texas Poet Laureate Series* (poems), TCU Press, Ft. Worth, Texas
2010: *The Skin of Light* (poems), Dalton Publishing, Austin, Texas
2011: *A Murder of Crows* (poems), Virtual Artists Collective, Chicago, Illinois
2013: *Uncle Ernest* (poems), Virtual Artists Collective, Chicago, Illinois
2014: *The Lobsterman's Dream (Poems of the Coast of Maine)*, El Grito del Lobo Press, Fulton, Missouri

Chapbooks

2001: *The Lighthouse Keeper* (poems), Timberline Press, Fulton, Missouri
2002: *The Woodlanders* (poems), Pecan Grove Press, San Antonio, Texas
2007: *With the Light of Apricots* (poems), Lily Press
2007: *Eros* (poems), *Slow Trains Literary Journal*
2008: *The Circus* (poems), *Right Hand Pointing*
2009: *Plain Pine* (poems), *Right Hand Pointing*
2010: *Dark Pearls* (poems), LaNana Creek Press (Stephen F. Austin State University), Nacogdoches, Texas
2010: *Wolves* (poems), El Grito del Lobo Press, Fulton, Missouri
2010: *Five Lavender Minutes of an Afternoon* (poems), *Right Hand Pointing*
2011: *The Red, Candlelit Darkness* (poems), El Grito del Lobo Press, Fulton, Missouri
2011: *Far* (West Texas) (poems), *Right Hand Pointing*
2012: *Social Networks* (poems), *Right Hand Pointing*
2013: *Colors* (poems), *Right Hand Pointing*
2014: *The Wadded Up Poem Behind the Dumpster*, *Right Hand Pointing*
2014: *The Goatherd*, Mouthfeel Press, El Paso, Texas
2014: *Art Museums*, Blue Horse Press, Redondo Beach, California

Acknowledgments

The author expresses special gratitude to Dr. Paul Ruffin, Director of Texas Review Press, without whose kindness and generosity this book would not exist.

The author further expresses gratitude to the editors of the following publications in which many of the poems in this book were first published, sometimes in slightly different versions:

Journals: *All Roads Will Lead You Home*, *American Indian Culture and Research Journal*, *Arkansas Review*, *Blue Rock Review*, *Blue Violin*, *Borderlands: Texas Poetry Review*, *Callaloo*, *Cenizo Journal*, *Chattahoochee Review*, *Concho River Review*, *Curbside Review*, *descant: fort worth's journal of poetry and fiction*, *DIN Magazine* (New Mexico State University), *Enigmatist*, *Green Hills Literary Lantern*, *Illya's Honey*, *Iron Horse Literary Review*, *JAMA: Journal of the American Medical Association*, *Langdon Review*, *Linnet's Wings* (Ireland), *Louisiana Literature*, *Midwest Quarterly*, *New Texas*, *Plainsongs*, *Poet Lore*, *Poetry Depth Quarterly*, *Radiant Turnstile*, *Rattle*, *REAL: Regarding Arts & Letters*, *Red River Review*, *Red Rock Review*, *Review Americana*, *Right Hand Pointing*, *Rio Grande Review*, *Riversedge*, *Ruminate Magazine*, *San Pedro River Review*, *Skive Magazine* (Australia), *Small Pond Magazine of Literature*, *Southwest Review*, *Southwestern American Literature*, *Sugar House Review*, *Sulphur River Literary Review*, *Texas Observer*, *Texas Review*, *Valparaiso Poetry Review*, and *Windhover*.

Anthologies: *Anthology of Magazine Verse & Yearbook of American Poetry*, 1997 edition, Monitor Book Company; *Beyond Forgetting: Poetry and Prose about Alzheimer's Disease*, The Kent State University Press ("Alzheimer's" published with the title "Diminuendo"); *Meow*, Outskirts Press ("Bobcat" published with the title "Feral Cat"); *Pushing the Envelope: Epistolary Poems*, Lamar University Press; *Texas in Poetry 2*, Texas Christian University Press; *The Weight of Addition*, Mutabilis Press; and *You Should Know*, Bunchgrass Press.

The selected poems herein previously appeared in the following collections: *Amazing Grace*, Texas Review Press, 2001; *Where Skulls Speak*

AS IF LIGHT ACTUALLY MATTERS

NEW & SELECTED POEMS

LARRY D. THOMAS

Texas Review Press
Huntsville, Texas

FIRST EDITION

Requests for permission to acknowledge material from this work should be sent to:

Permissions
Texas Review Press
English Department
Sam Houston State University
Huntsville, TX 77341-2146

Cover Art and Design: Nancy Parsons
Author Photograph: Lisa P. Thomas

Library of Congress Cataloging-in-Publication Data

Thomas, Larry D., 1947-
   [Poems. Selections (Texas Review Press)]
   As if light actually matters : new and selected poems / Larry
D. Thomas. -- Edition: first.
      pages cm
   ISBN 978-1-68003-024-2 (pbk. : alk. paper)
   1. Texas--Poetry. I. Title.
   PS3620.H63A6 2015
   811'.6--dc23
                                    2015003443

For my wife, Lisa

&

for my daughter, Deena

Contents

New Poems

from *Amazing Grace*

from *Where Skulls Speak Wind*

from *Stark Beauty*

from *The Fraternity of Oblivion*

from *Larry D. Thomas: TCU Texas Poet Laureate Series*

from *The Skin of Light*

from *A Murder of Crows*

from *Uncle Ernest*

from *The Lobsterman's Dream (Poems of the Coast of Maine)*

from Chapbooks: *The Circus*, *Plain Pine*, *Five Lavender Minutes of an Afternoon*, and *The Red, Candlelit Darkness* (complete)

The Circus

AS IF LIGHT ACTUALLY MATTERS

MATTERS

NEW & SELECTED POEMS

New Poems

Chiaroscuro

1. The Brighter the Sun

They boil their eggs in water
dashed with vinegar,
just to make the shells whiter.
Once or twice a year,
a bride dazzles the church
with the rare blinding snow
of her dress.

2. The Blacker the Shadow

Death ends their marriages.
They keep their flings
discreet as their envy.
Their Stetsons, Wranglers,
and Tony Lamas are black.
Clint Black croons on the radio.

3. Gray

in far West Texas
is anathema.
There's way too little rain.

Coyanosa

Its men eke out
a stark livelihood
from the dirty side
of oil, cotton, pecans,
and cantaloupes.

Its women bus their kids
twenty-six miles
to the nearest school,
and suckle infants
in never-ending galaxies

of drifting, ubiquitous dust.
"Far" is what they call
that part of West Texas.
South of town, rows of trees
at Wild Horse Pecan Farms

are ruler-straight
as the landowner,
Wild Horse the only thing
within hundreds of miles
resembling a bleak forest.

The hamlet's population
has shrunk to a dozen
cast-iron families stuck there
like filings flush against
a magnet of ancestors.

On Stationery of Light

I can't remember the last time
I penned a letter to a friend, in cursive,
but I would never have thought
that my next correspondence
would be this: printed with the pressing
of square, black keys on stationery
of light. But here it is, long after
the passing of much too many years.

I've lived in the Great Chihuahuan Desert
for two and one-half years now, perusing
a sky so blue, so vast, and so clean,
even of a wisp or two of clouds,
I find myself probing its depths
as one would a tome of philosophy.

The wind, though, in its myriad forms
often preempts the sky as my preferred
subject of inquiry: wafting, soughing,
and howling like a crazed prophet
long devoid the encumbrances of flesh,
so saturate with sun, moon, starlight,
and the desultory triad of death,
the buzz of flies, and history, he can't stop
the unremitting oozing of his prophecies.

Deep Woods

What sunlight crowbars through
appears in flashes, thin
as the beams of lasers.

What's not humus soon will be
in this place so humid
it's as if it's pelted

by a silent, endless rain.
Radiant in their oily,
bone china skin, their bodies

sixty-six percent water,
the woodlanders ease gecko-like
through the trail-less undergrowth

like translucent, white balloons,
water-filled, magical for a spell
with the blessing of flesh.

Lye Soap

(Deep East Texas)

For generations
they eked out their living
from the bottoms of the river
where nights came alive

with bellows of bull gators
and belches of marsh gas
bubbling to the surface
of reddish-black backwater sloughs.

For meat, they bled, dressed out,
and skinned whatever they could kill.
With lye from the ash of burnt wood
and razorback hog grease

boiled in a big black pot
till it thickened like jelly
for hardening in a pan,
they made their ugly soap

to camouflage, if only for
a moment, the musky,
ineradicable scent
of the bottoms.

The Draft

It has a sinister
air, troubled as the ghost
of someone murdered.
Each senses it
but dares not speak.
Rationalizing it

as a draft,
they rub their hands
and scoot a little closer
to the hearth.
Beyond the feeble reach
of reason,

brought to fruition
in the shadowy
purview of instinct,
it lurks, intransigent
as a pathogen
prying at a pore of health.

Cantaloupes

(far West Texas)

Nights, during
the picking season,
Ignacio
dreams orange dreams

of the fat,
ripe melons, snapping
from their stems
with the slightest

touch of his trembling
thumbs. Teeming
with the musky scent
of the melons,

Ignacio dreams,
clutching huge hands
rough and warty
as the rinds

of the melons.
He dreams of the fat,
numberless melons,
waiting under the thick,

heart-shaped leaves,
vying for the cool,
black shade
with diamondbacks.

In the Shade of My Neglect

The last time I noticed the rosebush,
in mid to late July,
it had conceded its foliage
to drought and black spot,
its lanky, four-foot stems
bleaching to beige and gray.

I gave it up for dead.
In the shade of my neglect,
in the silent wonder
of late summer rain
and imperceptibly
cooling temperatures,

it revived, quietly reclaiming
its former prominence
in the courtyard outside my studio.
This morning, goosed to brilliance
by the crystalline cattle prod
of the season's first cool front,

two rosebuds, swaying
in a shaft of sunlight,
caught the corner of my eye,
unfurling one by one
their silken petals, erecting
their delicate cathedrals of yellow.

Even the Roses Are Ill

The neurotic sunlight,
prying through the foul, sienna sky,

snaps and cracks its fingernails.
With growths on their eyes,

the hawks ride the thermals,
keeping their terrible distances,

locked in their circular drifts
of sociopathy.

Floundering in the shadows
of their lofts, the urbanites sigh,

musing the degree of their depression.
Their cats are marvels of psychosis,

batting mice around
till they stop moving,

for nothing but the sake of murder.
The rats, saturate with squalor

in the sewers, wax paranoid,
cringing from beams of feeble light.

Even the roses are ill,
trembling in their manias of red.

Winter Trees

The sky is overcast, glaring,
as if God were holding the earth
uncomfortably close
to a giant fluorescent light.

In stillness they're suspended there,
bereft of a single leaf,
all bark and verticality,
their thick sap rumbling in their roots

like the crude of capped wells.
They loom like shirtless prisoners,
hoisted in shackles to their toe tips,
braced for the blue, inexorable

scourges of wind and ice,
assuaged but momentarily
with the unguentary
roosting of the vultures.

Housefly

On an anvil
of light,
with the iron

of iridescence,
her weightless wings
were forged.

Death
beguiles her so
she lays

in what it claims
her cherished eggs.
She's the woman

of the house
of ubiquity.
For her eyes

alone, Picasso
would have sold
his taurine soul.

Gecko

The silence
of intractable shadow
beguiles you.

The pupils
of your bulbous eyes
are vertical ellipses.

The adhesive disks
of your toes
allow you to scale glass

without the slightest slip.
You inhabit
the dark interiors

of our lives, traversing
in closed drawers
the cases of compact discs,

navigating the thunder
of Beethoven,
the ink black reaches

of Scriabin.
Light burns you
like acid.

Bobcat

Deep in deep East Texas, after the pines
have flung their shadows across the road
like holy water searing the flesh
of a child possessed of the devil;

after day dies and the moon's a ghoul
easing up the trees like luminous blight;
after even the crows yield their cawing
to a storm-tossed sea of fear and terror;

and after all sound is snuffed
save the muted pulse of animals,
only then will he rustle on the dead-
leaf-bed under the thicket,

flex paws silent as moonglow,
soft as clouds, and set them one
ever-so-imperceptibly before another,
taking his place in the night.

Puma, Cougar, Panther, Mountain Lion

Hancock Hill, on one of whose
northern flanks our house rests,
is not one but several hills
bunched together and separated
by arroyos choked with yucca,
cholla, prickly pear, and whitebrush.

Yesterday, two hikers emerged
from the arroyo near the dumpsters
beside our street, their eyes still wide
from their sighting of two fresh
mule deer kills a half-mile or so
from our house. Local naturalists,

they could tell by the way
the carcasses were ravaged
the kills were the work of a lion.
As they drove away, I pondered
the countless nights it must,
in hunger, have circled our acre,

inching silently through the darkness
on the pliant black pads of its paws,
the circles of its stealth shrinking
with each soft, deliberate step,
tightening the noose of wilderness
around the dewy-eyed throat of our sleep.

Wolf in the Rain

He's miles from his den
in a driving winter rain.
From their headwaters
of his skull and spine,
a thousand little rivers
run toward the earth,

rounding the warm boulders
of his eyes, the mossy
black stone of his nose,
pooling in the shallows
of his tongue spastic
with panting, sloshing

against his fangs, tracing
the heaving parentheses
of his ribs to drip
from his pendulous
genitals, saturating
the seeds of buttercups

packed beneath his paws
in the dark, wet earth,
endowing them with wolf-stench
and the promise of a spring
profuse with the silent,
yellow howls of their blooming.

Steers in Summer, Lowing

Against a backdrop of blue heaven
and mesas hot as blacksmiths' anvils,
still stunned by the musk of men
who castrated them as calves,

they blanket the bleak range
like an unrolled scroll of reddish-
brown parchment scrawled with a savage
calligraphy of horns. Tails lash

hides so sunstruck they're tanned
alive on racks of ribs
guarding hearts and the grand
bellows of lungs. The nubs

of grass they grind with giant molars
are but straw they burn to fuel
their hellfire breath. The lavenders
of the evening ahead are cool

foreshadowings of their fate
of cold storage lockers on whose dim
hooks they'll sway as sides of meat,
drooling the mouths of those who fed them.

The Goatherd's Fingers

They move
a dark palimpsest
of his labors,

more the cloven hooves
of animals
than the tender

appendages of men.
Even in his sleep
they move,

as if to the muted
drums of his dreaming.
They tremble

in the moonglow,
warmed by the ragged
bellows of his breath,

redolent
with the musk
of teat and udder.

Munificence

(the goatherd muses)

Their udders house miracles
of milk, butter, and cheese.

Their dung is my fuel;
their flesh my seldom meat.

Their skins clothe me.
With their bones, I make

my simple tools. Their horns
are spoons; symbols of plenty.

The walls of their bowels,
sliced thinly into strips,

serve as sutures; string
cellos, violins.

Curandero

(a man who practices folk medicine)

Hiking deep
in the Sierra Madre,
I came upon the viejo
so abruptly he seemed
to appear from nowhere.

He reeked of the sheep
and goats he tended,
and had but one good eye,
his other an empty socket
filled with shadow.

Riveting his eye
to the bridge of flesh
between my own,
rasping in broken English,
he said a man, like a beast,

did not what he wanted
but only what he must
to make it through the day
to perilous night.
As he spoke, I heard,

from far upwind,
destined to flakes of ruin,
huge cathedral bells
chiming like the ricocheting
moans of madmen.

Rudyard's Pub

Some say it's so authentically British
it must have been scooped intact
from the heart of old London
and shipped to its final resting place

in the shadows of downtown Houston.
The regulars flock there every Thursday,
assume their designated stools at the bar,
and watch the regular bartenders

top frosted mugs with the amber heads
of Guinness on draft,
drawn with unctuous perfection.
They keep the talk small

and they swill, snapping into place
the last stubborn pieces of their puzzles,
suturing their fractured lives
with, just a comfortable reach away,

the whoosh and thud of darts
penetrating the dense agave fibers
of the dartboards, soothing as the sound
of desire, consummated.

Sleepwalker

Mindless, as if a chunk
of night itself, he walks
oblivious to destination

and the momentary
sanctuary of a home.
The muscles of his legs

are heated pulleys
snug against the wheels
of darkness. In deep snow,

in a world whose whiteness
is broken but by the sudden
blue shadow of an owl,

he walks completely vulnerable
to moonglow and the unforgiving
rules of hunting.

Though his eyes are open,
he can't see. His ears twitch
to the music of stars in deep space

grinding on their axes.
He trusts the cold,
mute strangers of his feet.

The Teacher

When he imitates the blind
reading Braille, though he, himself,
can see, he closes his eyes,

tilts his head back, places
his index fingers side by side
and sweeps them through the air

as if conducting a score of music.
He says most students, at least
early on, get so hung up examining

the anatomy of individual dots
it stifles their sedulous progress;
that the most capable

see their quavering fingertips
as the slippered feet of dancers
gliding over a floor of points

to get the feel of pattern,
dissolving the monotony of dots
into washes of color.

Dark Horse

(for Deena)

The night is so black it breathes.
I feel your presence but can't see you.
I extend my arm into the darkness.

Our fingertips meet. I grasp your hand
and pull you to the back of the black beast
I have straddled bareback.

You lock your arms around my waist,
and lean your head into the wind.
We are indistinct from the black night

we ride into, the black night
ravishing with us and the beast.
We feel the bass drum heart of the beast,

beating with the pulse of each of us,
three hearts beating with a single pulse,
beating to the rhythm of a numinous song,

the song of you, me, and the beast,
quaking the black night
with beautiful thunder.

Jewel

When she lost her hair to chemo,
she scarfed her head with black cloth
peppered with skulls and joked
that she was Jean Lafitte's
last surviving relative.

During the radiotherapy
which followed, she mused the sun
rising inside the dark,
miraculous cells of her body,
willing the cancerous ones

to thin out and perish like clouds
in the wide blue sky of remission.
It's been twenty years
since the young doctor
clasped her hands and,

in a soft, slightly breaking voice,
diagnosed her cancer as terminal.
Nightly, after spending another day
as a volunteer at the hospice,
she pours herself a glass of wine,

eases her eighty-year-old body
gently onto the curved,
dependable slats of her rocker,
and fondles the dying day's minutes
like diamonds in a jeweler's cloth.

Pale Horse, Pale Rider

His sprawling spread
was first his grandfather's,
then his father's.
Striking it rich
on gas and oil,

he started buying up
original Remingtons
and Russells he hung
in the bright white room
of the ranch house.

Imperceptibly, in the course
of his collecting, he spent
more and more time
among his oils.
His flesh grew pale

from lack of sun,
pale as the beautiful
mount he rode bareback
in his daydreams
across the cactus-strewn

pastures of investiture
to the grassy, high desert
plain of things seen.
He spent his last
days languishing

beneath his paintings,
his gaunt body
a clump of grease, breathing,
smudged against the canvas
of his cot.

Signs

Moving slowly as the hour hand
on the antique grandfather clock,
two weeks have passed since his

late wife's memorial service.
Her house shoes are still shoved
slightly beneath the side of the bed

she always slept on, ready
for her feet. Her clothes still hang
in the closet, saturate with her scent.

Though she's gone, he senses
the signs of her presence everywhere,
strangely more palpable than his own.

The morning sun hurls its buckets
of light through the windows,
brash and indifferent as always.

Ghosts

As if our truths
are anything but stories,
we brush off
those who believe in them

as ignorant
or superstitious,
those who know
ghosts are only losses

passing in a rush
of air; those superior
to ourselves in intellect
who early in their reading

see science and faith
as bridges
to the precipice of myth;
who hear them in attics

and trace their forms
in the fabulous wood
of totems; who know
that flesh itself

is but a phantom
manifest, fodder
for the entombed growth
of hair and nail.

With a Chest of Wings, *Caliban in Blue*

(for Walt McDonald)

As a child, he spent hours on end
staring into the cloudless blue skies
above Lubbock, watching for hawks
riding thermals, their talons clutched
like nooses pulled taut.

In hard winters, he studied hawks
frozen upright atop fence posts,
their talons sunk a half-inch deep in cedar,
eyes locked wide-open,
beaks parted with bubbles of bloody ice.

He spent hours on end
watching and studying hawks,
as if he knew he would crouch one day
strapped inside the fuselage of a fighter jet,
a fighter jet nothing but a hawk itself

with plumes of gleaming metal,
whooshing through the skies of enemies,
positioning itself for a dog fight:
as if he knew, with luck and God's good grace,
he'd make it home again

only to dream of those who didn't,
the unlucky ones parachuting to the clutches
of Charlie, buddies with the eyes of hawks
locked wide-open, riveted
to their trembling, helmeted skulls.

Our Lady of Guadalupe

(Mexico City, Mexico)

The weight of a history
scrawled in rivers
of human blood
has creased her face
into folds of fleshed bronze.
Little more than a slowly

moving skeleton
clad in black cloth,
she's already traversed
hundreds of feet
of stone worn smooth
by her ancestors,

inching her pilgrimage
in the hot, Mexican sun
toward the shrine,
stopping now and then
not for the cowardice
of rest, but to strengthen

the silver cage
of her heart
with yet another cross,
her life so sacrificed
to her penitence
she uses her knees for feet.

The Dump

At the dead end of an old red road
meandering through the Alabama woods,
it lies under a canopy of kudzu.

Here, the king is indistinguishable
from the pauper, like the old Cadillac,
its cracked leather seat strewn with the scat

of possums, what's left of its radio
locked on the station of oblivion.
Beneath a stack of old tires, a deflated

balloon, punctured by a broken instrument
for blowing bubbles, gleams dully in the sun,
inches from a rust-encrusted pocketknife

indifferent to ruin as the gamut
of usefulness it ran in its day
from mumbletypeg to intricate carving.

Kimbell Art Museum

(Fort Worth, Texas)

Intrigued with the *silver*
aspect of Texas light,
the architect* abhorred
skylights and clerestory

windows. Natural light
enters through a two-
and-one-half-foot slit
at the apex of vaulted

ceilings; strikes convex,
perforated aluminum;
reflects onto curved
concrete; ricochets

off walls of travertine
and the warmth of an oak
floor; merges with light
from incandescent lamps;

and illumes, as if its oils
were still wet with freshness
and glowing from within,
La Tour's masterpiece**,

leaving the viewer complicit
in the dazzling trinity
of the cheat, the servant,
and the courtesan.

* Louis Kahn
** *The Cheat with the Ace of Clubs*

Church, Taos Pueblo

(photograph by Ansel Adams)

The shaman of eye,
aperture,
and negative,

in the mastery
of absence,
he intensifies

the teeming
presence
of Indians.

With a palette
solemnly
predominant

with blacks
and grays,
in thin lines

lasering façade
from firmament,
he lets the light

scream the acid
oracles
of the gods.

Shotguns, 1987

(oil and acrylic on canvas by John Biggers)

On the porches of cottages called "shotguns"
because all their rooms open one into the next
in a line from front to back, allowing the pellets
of a shell shot through the front door unblocked
passage through the back, stand five black women
cradling dollhouse likenesses of their cottages,

their faces resolute as carved, African masks.
The pots and tubs beside them herald the purity
of the practical, domestic acts of soap preparation,
the cooking of pork, infant bathing and even
the catching of evil. The cottages' clapboard siding
resonates with the corrugated surfaces of washboards

or the rungs of ladders ascending the rows of gables
stacked above the women in luminously outlined
triangles simultaneously two and three-dimensional,
all the way to the outstretched wings of birds,
far below which, on grandma's quilt, lie railroad tracks
shimmering in the numinous geometry of the angels.

The Security Guard

(The Menil Collection, Houston, Texas)

Every night, for decades,
he's had the whole place
to himself. He knows

each work with the intimacy
of close friendship, relishing
the impenetrable nuances

beyond the feeble reach
of his knowledge. Blind-
folded, he could identify

each canvas by its scent.
His sense of hearing
intensifies with each

passing night, alert
even to the soft collisions
of motes of dust. At times,

if he listens hard enough,
he can hear the slow,
deep breathing of the artists.

The Art Preparators

(Museum of Fine Arts, Boston, Massachusetts)

To ready masterworks
for an off-site exhibition,
they take deep breaths
prior to even touching
the frames. They treat

the deliberate gestures
of their fingers, snug
in latex gloves, as if
they were turning the frail
pages of the Gutenberg Bible.

They cherish the instruments
of their craft: the Oz Clips,
plastic wrap, tape, glass
for glazing, travel trays,
foam-lined storage crates,

and the intricacies
of moving and storing
the crates. Laboring
in the radiance of angels,
they secure the crates

gently in the temperature-
and-humidity-controlled
cargo space of the truck,
exhale their deep breaths,
drop to their knees, and pray.

Taos Light

Like moths
to a flame,
it drew artists
in droves, raising
to incalculable powers
their reds, blues,

and yellows,
exacting their flesh
for the oils
of their oeuvres,
those gaunt old masters
leaning on their canes,

thin as filaments
heating to incandescence,
hollow as the husks
of moths
strewn about the base
of a lamp.

His Hard Art

(in memory of Hart Crane)

chose him and made him so facile
in the musical juggling of words
he could only speak in verse.

With his scalpel of perception,
in dissecting evil,
he stumbled upon the bones

of Lucifer, the Angel of Light.
It drowned him like a thrashing kitten
in the black well of consciousness,

leaving him the claw of his pen
to climb his way out, opening
his eyes wide and crazing them

with glimmer. But the sheen of oil
spilled on the sea in the sun
was enough to kill him.

The Old Man and the Sea

(after Hemingway)

The deck of his drifting boat's
his last vestige of land.
His eyes of deepest blue

conspire with sea and sky
to make even higher the icy,
cobalt flames of his hell.

Beyond thirst and hunger,
his brain raging in his skull
a hurricane of tricks,

his thoughts but feeble waves
slapping against the door of death,
he enters a windless calm, musing

how each passing tick of the clock
cuts another facet in the dazzling
white diamond of his passage.

Harmonica

(also known as mouth organ)

Even its reeds are metal
cold as the sweat of fear.
In blue lounge light suffused

with smoke, it gleams
like a small bar of silver
on the seabed. Two hands,

each easily passable for Van Gogh's
peasant's shoe and one of which
stays poised to flutter like a dying

dove, for tremolo, cup it. Lips
scarred with the phantoms
of little cancers, close on a row

of metal holes, as sodden lungs,
rattling the shackles of a million
Camels, inhale and exhale tone.

Piano Tuner

(for Marilyn)

The tools of his trade
are unassuming and relatively

primitive. The stagehand
is his counterpart in drama.

In the shadows of architects,
for grand cathedrals of sonatas,

he lays the bricks. Of pitch
and tone, he is master.

Even a concert pianist
steers clear of his ear.

from *Amazing Grace*

"Of Dust Thou Art"

In Van Horn, in far West Texas,
the sun has turned their faces
into deep red leathery brains.
They breathe dry air laden with red earth,

their lungs the lower halves
of rubbery hourglasses
turning year by sedulous year,
right before their eyes, into dust.

Even the hard oaken pews
they sit on during worship are dust-filmed
where they wheeze with clotted breath
the strains of "Amazing Grace."

Evenings, after the sun
has wobbled like a glob
down the rock-and-cactus-fleshed slopes
of mountains their forebears named "Diablo,"

they take to their gritty beds,
ease the quilts of grandmas
over their leathery bodies
like slabs of red earth, and they pray.

The Red Raging Waters

For weeks on end it has rained in Texas
sending the Brazos miles beyond its banks
where it rises even now under dark Texas skies

over the wooden floor of a bottomland Baptist church,
floating creaking pews shaped with the aching buttocks
of generations, the wild Brazos rising higher yet

to the stained-glass robes of the Apostles,
soaking the feet of Jesus and lapping the elbows
of His uplifted arms, creeping up the pulpit

on whose open Bible coils a fat diamondback,
the red raging waters of the Brazos
bringing to sweet communion the serpent and the saint.

String Cadenza

The cowhand's
sun-and-ice-lined face,

its features
harsh and sharpened
like a wind-hewn peak,

reeks of half-cooked
barbecued brisket.

His fingers are stiff
from castrating calves
in the cold,

his legs bowed
to the great rib cage
of a quarter horse

whose savage hairs
string the bows of violins.

Primary Colors

(for Deena, in memory of Edith Thomas)

For several months,
Mom's clinical depression
had kept her indoors.
She killed time
drifting through her universe

of drugs, clad
in but her gown
and pale blue housecoat
she kept buttoning
below her knees, for prudence.

One late October day,
after a blue norther
had passed through town,
rubbing the sky
to raw cobalt,

my daughter of three
led her by her pinkie
to the backyard,
got her to lie down
in the grass,

and buried
all but the cameo
of her face
under a foot or more
of red and yellow leaves,

believing,
with all her heart,
that that many reds and yellows
couldn't help but thaw
her Grandma's blues.

Fox Fire

(deep East Texas)

After weeks of light rain
the floor of the woods
is sodden as a bog,

a patchwork of oxblood
and mustard tallow leaves
disintegrating from the thread-

like skeletons of their veins
in the black machinations
of rot, scat-scented,

shining with frog-slime, upthrust
by the shoots of mushrooms
muscling their way through the mire,

loosing old fox-stink
to slither through the mist
like warm steam.

The Slough

The decaying pine boards of his porch
creak beneath the rockers of stained oak
shaped by the hands of his father.
He kills his time there, rocking,

staring deep into the woods
of his grandfather, toward the slough.
For ten years, since he turned seventy,
it's risen in the basement of his dreams.

The haven of gator and cottonmouth,
it's harbored for three generations
his clan's deepest secrets. Late at night,
if he listens hard enough, he can hear

the muffled, steady engine of its rot.
It works its timeless wonders
under still, dark waters. Its film
has already claimed his pale, blue eyes.

Late Sonata

For sixty years a teacher of piano
and well into her eighties,
she wakes into the glory

of another spring,
pressing white fingers
deep into dark potting soil

as she plants a geranium
shaking its scarlet fists.
Her hearing aid's

percussive with the dissonance of jays
dripping through budding oak branches
like pints of spilled blue paint.

As she tamps the damp soil,
her mind turns
to the cool ecstasy of evening

when her fingers will flutter
over a keyboard of wisteria,
seeking choice flowers she'll pluck,

dip in fresh batter,
and fry for a light evening meal
of fragrant lavender.

Of Eyes Wondrously Wild

(for Lisa)

Clawing the street
under the tree of its birth,
it lay there on asphalt
cooling with shadows of evening.
Limp at its side

hung its broken wing
auguring hidden injuries
ridiculously accidental
and far too soon, fatal.
I eased it with great care

to the cupped left hand
of my wife. With her right
index finger she stroked it
in a futile human attempt
to soothe the dark terrors

of eyes wondrously wild
for the fleeting little seconds
of a life. It blinked
once or twice, shuddered, and died,
her cupped hand its warm coffin.

My wife's eyes watered
and a breeze came,
lifting her hair from her cheeks
like the soft glorious wings
of ascension.

Mooring Line

(West Beach, Galveston Island)

Pearled with barnacles,
it lies half-buried in the dunes
like the necklace of a giant,
flung angrily to the ground.

Braided with thick,
blue and white strands of nylon,
its ends are frazzled
as an old maid's hair, scorched

from one too many permanents.
Its massive size belies its weakness,
its nylon long ago compromised
by sun and weeks on end at sea.

With nothing to show it mercy
but the laggardly deepening sand,
it'll lie this way for months,
sponging the screams and fleeting

shadows of the gulls,
tethering uselessness
to the slow, consuming pull
of ruin.

Still Water

Once I saw the Gulf
flat as a mirror
of silvery,
imperceptible waves.

From where I stood,
squinting in the sun,
I saw not sea
but firmament

replete with pelicans.
Two lovers bathing
stood waist-deep in clouds
and splashed themselves

with heaven. Several
yards out, in their dinghies,
the men were rapt, casting
either nets or ashes.

The Light of Mexico

It's no wonder the painters
revere it so; the way,
in little villages,
it brings out the pinks, greens,

blues, yellows, and lavenders
of humble houses
dazzling the flanks of mountains
like strewn fruit; the way,

at zero hour, suits of it
mesmerize the eyes of bulls;
the way, as if from nowhere,
it sparkles the dark,

chocolate eyes of mothers
so comfortable with death
they candy its skulls
for the tongues of bronze children.

from *Where Skulls Speak Wind*

Wind

(circa 1880, West Texas)

It died down to a zephyr
but would never, never stop.
All they did was listen
and grace it now and then
with psalms and gospels.
Its dogged struggle

was a perfect metaphor
for their faith, the manner,
even for their memory,
in which it kept after them,
sanding their gravestones
night and day to dust.

When the sky greened and it rose,
in case it made a cyclone,
they grabbed their kids and hurried
down the steps of their cellars,
armed with but hard prayer
to foil the howling darkness.

Antique Shop, After Closing

This place, after closing,
is hushed as the tomb
of a Pharaoh,

this place of objects
complete in themselves,
shrine-like,

beyond the selfish reach
of usefulness,
like poems

deconstructed
into the bleached,
wooden blocks

of an alphabet
randomly strewn
on a shelf in a place

where nothing moves
but light, shadow,
and dust drifting

downward through the darkness
like the laying on
of hands.

Road Kill

It's as if they lay there
in the pattern of some dark plan,
spaced as they were on the macadam,
flattened by the sole of a jealous god
for imminent mummification by the sun,
a male and female jackrabbit
catching the corner of my eye at daybreak.

I couldn't help but picture the instant
before their deaths, their eyes all pupil
leading them through the ink black night,
making sudden contact with beams
so bright they had to be celestial,
leaving them hopelessly paralyzed
in the snapshot-quick of rapture.

A Place in the Sun

When a dutiful child,
I sat on my pew with folded hands
like a strange piñata
layered with the onion-
skin pages of my Bible.

As I grew up, the layers
dried and cracked wide-open,
oozing the pungent
smelling salts of recognition,
drawing me up, against my will,

in the middle of communion,
from the hard oaken pew
of my chrysalis
and leading me up the aisle
and outside to take my rightful place

in the sun, shocking the congregation
with my ostensible irreverence
though I stood in the bright hot light
more consonant with Jesus
than I'd ever been.

The Night We Were Gods

They hung by thread
just above our heads
in the kitchen entryway,
five hummingbirds
of clear red glass

covered with glitter.
Absentmindedly,
we brushed them
with the tips
of our forefingers,

rubbed our eyelids,
and smeared them
with galaxies
of tiny stars.
For several hours,

till we showered,
and never even
noticing, we blessed
everything we touched
with crushed light.

Bluing

It came in a little
bottle, so blue it looked
jet-black. I knew it was
nothing but trouble,
the way a tiny

drop of it would turn
a washtub of water
into a huge, sloshing
sapphire. Mama used it,
oddly enough, to whiten

our Sunday shirts.
Over time it bled
right through her skin
and blued her all the way
to commitment

in the Wichita State
Hospital, bleaching
her heart into a locket
white and fragile
as fine bone china.

Grandmother Thomas

(in memory of Issiebell Wright Thomas)

She came to live with us
shortly before she died.
Her skin tone was brown
as the cotton stockings
whose tops she rolled down
just below her knees.
She had high cheekbones,

angular as the rest
of her tall, gaunt frame.
At least half-Indian,
she cringed when asked
about her bloodline,
whether she were Cherokee
or some other tribe.

She'd been taught that they
were savages, half-human;
that she should deny
an ounce of their blood.
Nights, when her bedroom
light went out, I'd creep
to her door, lie down, and listen

with my ear to the space
beneath the door.
I'd hear her muffled
chanting, oozing like the coos
of doves, the Great Spirit
washing over me
like mild fever.

Mule Trader

(in memory of Charles Franklin Thomas)

Before his retirement,
his knobby fingers reeked
of the drool of mules
whose mouths he pried open
to glance at their teeth,
extracting their age
to perfection. In his
golden years, too old
to fiddle with the mouths

of mules, he whittled cowboys
with his pocketknife
from thin, flat pieces
of pine. He'd suspend them
on twisted cotton string
between two sticks
joined by a brace
at their centers. When one
squeezed the sticks, the cowboys

flipped back and forth
like acrobats,
as if he knew
the time would soon come
when the valiant
cowboy of his youth
would pass to legend,
put out to the pasture
of tricks and movies.

The Cisco Kid

(in memory of Margaret Ann Elizabeth Coleman)

It came on the same time
each week, Mama Sug's
favorite Western TV show.
She'd get so excited
watching it, Mother
was concerned for her heart.

I'll never forget the way
she riveted her pale blue eyes
to the black-and-white screen,
squinting to see the characters,
the bad cowboys in black hats,
the good ones in white.

Though the good guys always won,
one would never have known it
by watching Mama Sug,
tense as a convict
in the electric chair,
waiting for the flip of the switch.

After she fell and broke her hip,
it was the only thread
that pulled her from one
brutal week to the next.
I didn't know till she died
her maiden name was Cisco.

Jake

(in memory of Rufus Andrew Coleman)

He and Mama Sug
passed their idle time
fishing tanks with cane poles
for crappie and perch.
His back bowed from years
of plowing fields with mules
and fathering ten children,
he never complained
and hardly ever spoke.

Though he had but one good lung,
I never saw him sans
a hand-rolled cigarette
dangling from his lips,
lumpy as Mama Sug's
homemade soap. For forty years,
after she got religion,
Mom hounded him
to get baptized. Finally,

just before he died
at eighty-five, to shut
Mom up, he gave in
and was dunked. As soon
as he got home, he rolled
himself a Prince Albert
and snuck a swig of Old Crow
he'd kept hidden for years
for such a sweet occasion.

Alzheimer's

She first heard its onset
in the sudden, *staccato*
rhythm of her speech,
in the gradual diminishing
of brilliant memory

from chord to *arpeggio.*
Though largely confined
to the minimalist composition
of her nursing home room,
she still insists that the aide

help her daily with a black gown
and wrap her hair in a bun.
Positioned on her bench
with the straight-backed posture
she assumed as a concert pianist,

she sits at her only window
and watches the *diminuendo* of light
from afternoon to evening,
evening to dusk and dusk
to the endlessly repeated

étude of the night,
each of her long,
slender fingers
swaying like the winding down
needle of a metronome.

from *Stark Beauty*

The Skull Seller

(Terlingua, far West Texas)

She said she'd lived
there all her life.
As she spoke, a wisp
of white dust engulfed us,

brushed from the skulls
of steers she scoured
for bleaching by the sun.
Her eyes were the palest

blue I'd ever seen,
bleached as the skulls
tagged and shelved for sale.
She rambled on about

the vast Chihuahuan
Desert, how it baked them
in the low-heat oven
of the sun, leathering

flesh over time
for rasping by the ever
present wind, for the rasping
of their skulls to mortars,

their bones to pestles
pounding them down
to the powder
of blinding light.

Texas Mountain Laurel

In early spring,
for a distance
of several feet,

it wafts the aroma
of the thick, sweet
juice of grapes.

Its branches creak
and sway, laden
with the cascading

clusters of blooms
teeming with bees
like monks in amber

robes, intoxicated
with contemplation,
humming their chants,

rapt in fragrant
monasteries
of lavender.

Cotton

It blanketed Mother
in the pale blue
softness of a nightgown;
Dad, the propriety
of a white shirt.

At their request,
even their caskets
were fashioned of it
to aid their swift
reunion with the earth.

For miles around
the cemetery,
red fields of it
lay fallow, fields
where in their youth,

sunup to sundown,
they picked it, each
a hundred pounds a day,
where they picked it
till their fingers bled.

The Vacant Lot

It loomed across the alley
which ran beside the parched
West Texas sandboxes
our parents called their yards

like a small, unspoiled
parcel of Chihuahuan Desert.
As kids, we'd hike its narrow
trails, dodging prickly pear,

yucca, and branches of lithe
mesquite camouflaging thorns,
careful not to step on ants,
horned frogs or scorpions.

Near its center, hidden
beneath a copse of mesquite,
between two little sand dunes
where not even the roving

eyes of mothers could spot us,
we'd face our heartthrobs
with the wide-eyed, breathless
spasms of our bodies,

fondling their every nook
for the dark, forbidden
facts our fathers hinted at
but hadn't yet let us in on.

Harvest Moon

for Deena

It hung in the late
October sky
so big and bright
people everywhere,
just to look at it,
pulled their cars
over to the shoulders
of the roads.

My daughter of two,
clung to my chest
like a monkey,
caught suddenly up
in the throes
of her small body
acting with a mind
of its own, pointed her right

index finger toward the sky,
parted her pursed lips,
and crooned, for the very
first time, sliding off her tongue
like a warm, sweet disk
of butterscotch candy,
the word, "moon," startling
her so she started crying.

Drovers

they were called
by the trail boss,

just dollar-
a-day drovers

content to subsist
on biscuits,

bacon,
beans and,

if lucky, a slurp
or two of syrup,

the cattle
they wrangled

too valuable
at the railhead

for racks of ribs
or brisket

on the trail,
just dollar-

a-day drovers
driving herds

from Texas
up to Kansas

for months, up
to where a month's

pay fizzled
to bottles

of rotgut
and slipshod

quarter-hours
with a whore.

From the Faraway Nearby

(oil on canvas by Georgia O'Keeffe)

The residue
of a life fully lived
intrigued her more
than the living,
the residue

of color, skull,
shape and antler
never far away
as vista and vast,
unreachable sky,

distance she knew
she could dwarf
with but a thing nearby
like this gracefully
antlered skull

rendered so dominant
against a backdrop
of sky and far
away hills. She knew
she could snag the far

with the near
by nudging the tip
of the uppermost antler
just beyond the canvas
edge. So she did.

Bones

O'Keeffe found them
left so immaculate
by the sun and wind
it was as if someone,
with bleach and the bristles
of a steel brush,

had scoured them clean.
In the winter of her life,
as she strolled the desertscapes
of Ghost Ranch with her cane
and beloved black chow chow,
she must have felt her own

reaching for the light, pressing
against her skin from within,
seeking in the clear
New Mexican air the music
of radiant bleaching
by the sun.

Western Artist

From the sang-froid
of slaughter,
he extracts
his viscous red.

For his yellow,
with his cupped hand,
he scoops
the fiery

butter
of the sun.
Of the thud
of hawk

against dove,
in the deep,
resultant bruise,
he finds his blue.

from *The Fraternity of Oblivion*

Rite

In late night fog
his eyes mist
beneath black goggles
for the imminence

of his colors.
Close behind him
on his wide-
open Harley

rides his woman,
musing her fate
as a chapter sheep.
He'll share her

in the dunes
with each dark stranger,
and already sees
clusters of hard stars

churning in turn
in the winged skull
of each moonlit back
and their sheep-woman

rising from the dunes,
sown with the rich,
chapter seed
of blood brethren.

A Brother

He wakes
before the others
in the sharp shadow
of his Harley.
The broken
driftwood logs
still smolder.

Another log breaks,
and he remembers
how they broke his legs
for snitching off
a brother.
All around him
and the others,

the ghost crabs,
poised at the mouths
of their foxholes,
glare at him
with the black
lidless eyes
of allegiance.

The Tribe

They once killed a night
and skinned it
for their clothing.
They stop
for another night

at a roadside park
in the pines.
It has just rained,
and the whole place
reeks of fresh resin.

The moon is nothing
but a globe
of luminous
violence.
They start a fire

and sit around it
like a tribe
of whiskered Indians,
listening for owls.
They speak in soft tones.

Just feet away
the cold, black shadows
of their Harleys
flicker like a swarm
of giant, iron ants.

They Left His Face

a mesh of red welts.
They left him
for dead
in the bar's dark

parking lot
where he wakes
but can't move,
his denim vest stuck

to the black bloodstains
of old Harleys.
He still feels
the frigid metal

of each thick chain.
Yet another tooth
dribbles from his lips,
and he grunts

a scant smile
just for the colors
he shielded,
till he lost

consciousness,
with jutting,
shattered
shoulder blades.

Procession

They ride
in solemn pairs
in the dazzle
of bright sunlight.

Sweat stings
black-sunglassed eyes,
trickles through thick
beards, and beads

in the cracks
of tattooed skulls.
They ride
behind the black hearse

of their leader.
Beneath lean,
black-clad buttocks
the big bikes rumble

like a procession
of dark bull fiddles
sobbing in the clutches
of their prodigies.

The Black Hearts

Nights,
the moon hovers in the sky
like a blood-gorged mosquito,
and dances in the studs
of black wristbands.

Black hearts beat
under black vests
of thick leather.

They ride
only at night
and split the dark
like sledge-driven wedges.

Days,
they scrape
from under their nails
the black, caked blood
of iron hogs.

At Perfect Ease

A Harley's killed
for the night
at a roadside park,

the moon
a yellow maniac
raving in the irises

of plumed eyes;
a biker
covering himself

with the orchestrated fumes
of old bedding
as owls

for miles and miles around
swoop down on frenzied shrews;
a biker falling asleep

at perfect ease
with this violent
scheme of things.

The Virtuosa

having raked sex
of love
and all its other
accoutrements,

paints her last nail
with shiny,
jet-black polish.
She has honed her soul

to a pure, hard art.
She stares
at the sharp profile
of her body

in a cracked mirror,
and marvels
at her mastery
of line

in breast, belly, butt,
each a perfect
measure
of her lust.

A Pierced Ear

hears the heavy breathing
of brothers
waiting in the dark.
A brain burns time
like fresh fuel,
each lobe a Harley's

revved up piston.
Hair's butchered.
A shaved face is shocked
with artificial light,
flesh red and raw
from scouring.

But hours ago
a hot shower
scalded weeks
of cultivated grime.
A groin still smarts
with burning ointment.

The Man stripped him
of everything he could,
everything but his prized,
black tattoos with which
he hunkers down in the cool,
green sanctum of his cell.

from *Larry D. Thomas: TCU Texas Poet Laureate Series*

In the Voodoo Lounge

An hour after showtime,
the lights go out.

An old black man
navigates the glow
of black lights,
and eases his buttocks
to the woven
cane bottom of a chair.

His knobby,
sharecropper fingers
clutch a pick
and curl
around the long,
fretted neck
of his Fender.

A riff
surges through the darkness
like neon gas
through a glass tube.

One by one,
fierce black lions
leap from the steel
of plucked strings,
ripping sodden hearts
with the unsheathed
claws of the blues.

Twin Spinsters in Blue

It's an early
December morning
an hour before sunrise.
The quiet streets
of Cherryhurst Park

are completely canopied
with the branches of oaks
hundreds of years old.
Their long blue-black coats
sashed at their waists,

they sit at the center
of the park in the sun,
their navy blue canes
angled against their bench.
They can count

on their gloved fingers
the words which pass between them,
having long survived
the last of their living kin.
They spend their days this way,

acting out the script of simple ritual,
the deep sky above them
familiar at last
as the blue silk handkerchiefs
creased inside their purses.

The Laws of His Kind

are mutable as the changing faces
of the alpha males.
His gravestone but the camouflage
of a thick blanket

of loblolly needles,
he lies like a mummy
in a wrap of doeskin
bound by the calloused hands

which stilled his breathing.
He lies under several feet
of the rich, black humus
they're all destined to,

staring down the darkness
with his three, wide-open eyes,
his mercifully orchestrated death
eternally uncertified as his birth.

In the Nacreous Hours

(September 1900, Galveston, Texas)

before the Great Storm of 1900,
a calm breeze rustles palm fronds
like cotton castanets. The evening sky
is opalescent, disturbed by nothing

but the glides, swoops, and dives of gulls.
The children are nonchalant,
licking their bright red lollipops,
stuffing their mouths with sticky

pink wads of cotton candy.
The waves, grown mysteriously angry,
strike shell beds with the opening notes
of Beethoven's *Fifth*. The puppet limbs

of lovers are thrashing in the sky,
the cotton threads of their lifelines
twisting, fraying, held by but the screaming
of the brute, careening gulls.

Bach

Encircled
by a baroque design
of oak leaves, acorns
and flowers, his profile's

tooled in brass,
centered in a small
brass plate hanging on the wall.
He faces east, his gaze

fixed on something elusive,
contrapuntal as the melody
of light pouring in daily
through the window,

juxtaposed with shadow
in a silent fugue
building to the climax
of the night.

Flaking the Slate Gravestones

This Sunday morning in October
a dense fog has settled over Boston
like gray gauze damp with ether,

eased to the breathing of the ill.
I make my way by foot to Cambridge Street,
and I see the street people,

a white man, a black woman,
making love on a concrete mattress
under a tattered gray blanket,

barely moving as I pass yet making love
as if nothing else matters,
neither the nearby Common of Lowell's ". . . Union Dead"

nor the cascading chimes of Park Street Church
drifting through the mist to Granary Burying Ground,
jarring the bones of Revere, Hancock, Adams,

flaking the slate gravestones
with the rhythmic, invisible chisel
of the hymn.

French Quarter

(New Orleans, Louisiana)

(for Deena)

Below sea level, in night fog
thick as chicken and sausage gumbo, it looms,
this whole place a brick and concrete grave
adorned with Spanish and French iron,
a grisly Easter basket

wrapped in alternating bands
of green, gold, and purple cellophane
under which flicker the lights,
the ghastly lights of gas lamps and neon
every hue of the rainbow

illuming the ghostly faces
of voodooienne Marie Laveau
and the Saint Louis Cathedral
sticking its spires into night sky
like pins in a doll of voodoo, voodoo

whose rhythmic chants gave birth to jazz
in this glittering city of sin and Lent
forever gently nudged by the giant python
of the Mississippi: triumphant, tumescent,
and shining from its meal of mice and men.

The Dragonfly

Through the glass I see a radiant hue.
Inside my writing studio vacant
for several days, a hot shaft of sunlight,
shining through a skylight, illumes the blue
husk of a dragonfly. Last week it flew
into the room. I never noticed it.
All I know is when I left, it didn't,
but died of old age or starvation, too

feeble to last till I returned and dart
for the aperture to sky when I slid
the glass door open. Now, but its blue glows,
emptied of the juice of life, the hard art
of its karma gaudy as the eyelids
of harlots, slathered with sparkling shadow.

Crow with Red Sky

(watercolor by Leonard Baskin)

Grossly oversized,
fashioned from the grunts of gods,
its legs are blunt pedestals
for the black marble density

of a body usurping a backdrop
of red sky so violently
its tail's chopped off by the paper's edge.
Its beak's a stubby holocaust

of buffed, black iron.
Black hairs jut from feet and legs
like rebar tips in cured concrete.
It stands on a flat surface

balanced on the points of eight claws
etched with the strength to pierce steel.
All of heaven sparkles
in the closed, black noose of its eye.

Minotaur

Though his hands,
by turns,
can chisel *David*
from marble
and execute

the ravishing,
intricate scores
of Beethoven,
he would trade
a thousand

for a single
cloven hoof
to paw the blood-
soaked earth
of a bullring,

his bull's
dark desire
languishing
in the paltry,
flaccid organ

of a man,
ridiculous
for placating
even the gentlest
cow in heat.

from *The Skin of Light*

The Winter Sky

is overcast, the ice-glazed parchment
of yellow grass beneath it

dramatic with Rorschachs of crows.
I think of Lowell

running naked through the snow
of Harvard Yard, headed nowhere,

manic, a chunk of red meat
reeking for the talons of a raptor,

reeling in the eloquent,
skunk-stench hell of his Self.

Gibbous Moon

Slowly above
the ridge
it rises,

convex
with shadow,
breaking

through clouds,
almost full,
the way

my first two
marriages
almost lasted;

the way music,
art museums
and poems,

convex
with shadow,
will shed

the skin
of light
I'll need

to almost
get me
through the night.

As If

The dusk reddens, its chafed flesh
pulsing above the tightened noose
of darkness. The icy wind
rips at the breasts and wings of grackles,

mad for the flutes of their hollow bones.
Its chill, near freezing as they spiral
down from the sky by the thousands
to roost, will drop to single digits

by midnight. Though hundreds of them,
exposed for hours to sleet and bitter cold,
will die well before sunrise,
each, for all it's worth, clutches its twig

and ruffles its blue-black feathers,
as if it will make it; as if it knows
the *as if* is all it's ever had
to stagger it to daybreak.

Dying Vulture at Sundown

I came upon it in a pasture
in the middle of nowhere,

thinking at first it lay dead.
Too weak to stand, it raised its head

hooded with tufts of red flesh, looked
me in the eye, and blinked.

Showing neither fear nor any hint
of struggle, it stretched out its wings,

sank their tips into the desert,
and pulled them like black oars,

easing the rowboat of its body
through the shadowy waters

which, all its fetid existence,
had charmed and nourished it.

The Crow

is all I know,
a path so black
it's tinged with blue.
I set out on it
years ago, at dusk.

Each step I take
is quickly
smothered with brambles.
I know not
where the path began,

just that it runs
crooked before me,
and has no end.
I savor the stench
fuming from the hour

of night. Carrion
fuels the throbbing
engine of my heart.
My feathers are quills
sopping with the ink

of my blood, stuck
in the parchment
of my fetid flesh.
I keep the earth clean.
On death alone

my dark kind fattens.
I roost in dead trees,
gurgling the bold,
black poem
of my Self.

Sparrow Egg

To allow
its quiet making,
a mother blinks,
folds her wings,
and lets her body

work, pulsing
with the tiny,
velvet hammers
of the angels.
Once it's perfect,

from its yolk
of golden awe
to the pale,
yellowish-white
of its covering,

she lays it
in an airy fold
of her bill-
woven tapestry
of grass.

Fabergé
labored decades
to execute
a semblance
of its shell.

Mayflies

Imagine a day
so holy with light
its hours are years,
a single day
whose morning is the youth
and evening the autumn
of entire lives.

Imagine these creatures
so taken with this day
they desire no other,
so ephemeral
even a mouth
would be extravagant;
these creatures

who find fulfillment
in their first
and only sunrise,
their daylong lives
satiate with a single
act of love
before drifting

softly downward
to their dying,
leaving, even
in their deaths,
the rivers scintillant
with the gossamer
of wings of light.

Apache Child

(Mescalero Apache Reservation)

Her braids are so black
they're tinged with blue,
gleaming with the sheen
of ravens
careening in sunlight.
Each Sunday,
for ten new words
of her ancestral tongue,
she treks to the prefab,
government-issued shanty
of her great-grandmother,

sits on her lap,
and fixes herself
in a trance.
From the shriveled,
quavering lips
of the matriarch,
the sacred words
whoosh like falcons
thrown upon the wind.
The new word-falcons
tethered to her wrist,

she heads for home
and the night when,
her bronze face
cradled in the down
of her pillow,
she'll mouth the words
over and over

till she owns them,
each a priceless glass bead
added to the bracelet
of her soul.

Hot Pink, Day-Glo Chartreuse, and Electric Blue

(for Deena)

All of three, but a dozen feet
from the frothy, receding tongue
of the Atlantic, she's spent hours
working her hot pink plastic shovel,

scooping damp sand into her Day-Glo
chartreuse bucket, patting it flat
at the bucket's rim, then dumping it
behind the little dunes of her electric-

blue-bikini-clad butt. The gulls frolic
in a flock above her, mindless
in their joy as her blond, flopping pigtails.
She keeps straightening her bikini top

as if she needs it, working her sand
till sundown, sedulous in her efforts
as an elderly watchmaker, spellbound
with the intricate machinery of time.

Stained Glass

Its enamels were opaque
until 1650 when Johann Schaper
fashioned transparent ones

to allow the bleeding through of light.
After application,
to become one with the glass,

they were kiln-fired,
and exposure to the sun
for centuries

hasn't faded them.
They grace the windows of cathedrals
like molten jewels,

infusing the light with color
to flood the faces
of penitents rapt in prayer,

the light wafting through the air
like the dazzling cologne
of God.

The Miners

(in memory of Mark Rothko)

At daybreak, like swarms of upright ants,
they enter the lightless shafts,
pack dilapidated elevators
for passage to the depths of hell,

and brace themselves for their jobs of darkness.
As their fathers and grandfathers before them,
they'll take their picks to veins of anthracite
shining in their feeble light like late

Rothko canvasses* so close to their noses
they can smell them. As they pick
they'll breathe black dust filling the rattling,
rubbery hourglasses of their lungs.

For decades, they'll labor in blackness
vast as night, chipping away as if certain,
deep within its endless depths,
looms because it must a terrible beauty.

*Rothko Chapel, Houston, Texas

Black-on-Black

(by Maria and Julian Martinez, Pueblo potters)

The clay she sought was the very body
of her Mother Earth she dared not touch
prior to the utterance of prayer,
the offering of sacred cornmeal.
Only then did she work it

with the sure, muscular grace of her hands,
drying the raw clay to soak it
and sieve it clean with the woven sifter
of her grandmother, mixing it with a temper
of pure volcanic tuff.

Her hands met the clay on its own ancient terms
as it shaped itself with wet pieces of gourds
flush against her flesh, as it smoothed itself
with wet corncobs tickling the creases of her palms.
Dried leather-hard, the clay was ready for carving,

for brushstrokes of yucca soaked with black pigment
bled from the stems and leaves of the guaco,
polished to a sheen with smooth stones
and adorned with a pattern of feathers
Julian painted with a screened clay slip

for the early, windless morning of the firing,
the moment of truth when the clay burned
a bright cherry red and she smothered the fire
with the dung of sheep, horse, or cow,
letting the clay cool and rubbing it with fat for luster.

from *A Murder of Crows*

The Sparrow

By cold, hunger, or the brutal
amusement of a cat, it probably
will die before I do. It hops
easily its height, and quietly

explodes into flight to the nearby
branch of an evergreen. It jerks
into a shaft of winter sunlight,
flaunting for a moment its earth

tone browns and grays. Struck
by the dazzle of its dullness,
I muse its world where survival
by the minute is enough,

where contentment is an ounce
or two of trembling flesh,
a bundle of feathers, and tiny bones
hollow as its consciousness of loss.

Starlings

Their gurgled
birdsong
precedes them.

They descend
from the heavens
like shredded

midnight,
showering morning
with iridescent

black confetti.
By evening,
for an easy nest,

the chunky males
will grab
baby sparrows

by their necks,
drag them
from a birdhouse,

and drop them
to burst
like ripe figs.

Sturnus vulgaris.
Even their Latin
is vulgar.

Driftwood Gull

With nails of stainless steel,
it's fixed to the rail of a fence.
Days, sunlight and shadow
rake its knobbed circumference.

Nights, moons swathe it with the gauze
of moonglow. The sea's expectorant,
cured to the perfection
of hard silence, it looms pregnant

with the promise of its cry
locked in its throat like a rock of salt,
wretched life but whose form's eternal,
alien both to ruin and want.

Hawks

Gray clouds saturate with rain
hang so low in the sky they shroud
the tops of the dark winter trees
where they roost in solitude,

brandishing toward the interstate
the cream-colored shields of their breasts.
For several hours he's seen them
through the windshield of his Camry,

spaced every few miles at intervals
measured by the cold, aluminum
ruler of their need. He muses his wife
asleep in the passenger seat

beside him, his wife of twenty years
who two years ago ended
and confessed her brief affair,
the wife he thought he knew but didn't.

He muses the precise intervals
of her slow, guiltless breathing,
the aquiline silhouette, both strange
and familiar, of her profile.

Raptor

(Golden Eagle, far West Texas)

The bleak Trans-Pecos
is his kingdom. On a ledge
high above the sun-baked
bounty of the desert, he sledge-

hammered the shell
of his birth egg, and, protean,
sucked from the wind
its savage cerulean

scream. With reckoned abandon,
deep into God's eye he hurls
the slingshot pellet of his body
to soar in fierce thermals,

deft at tearing out hearts,
rending God's stead
asunder with the arrow
of his golden head.

Raven Is His Favorite Verb

Fetid breath fumes from his beak,
the price he pays for acumen
in the commerce of death.

Raven is his favorite verb,
transitive, the carcass heart
as desirous a direct object

as the plump, ripe berry.
He has no friends or loved ones,
just the urge to caw, soar, and rend,

the thin volume of hell
irrelevant to his blue-black oeuvre
as the even thinner one of heaven.

Crow

History reeks
of the ineradicable
blackness
of your ink.

As metaphor,
for thousands
of years,
you've charged

our psyches,
forging
the dark iron
of your being

into symbols
of life, death,
and the scales
of justice.

Higher
and faster
than all
other birds,

you fly.
Your caw
still ices
our sodden hearts.

Both the Proposition and the Proof

The carrion
the crow relishes
is his mockery
of death.

Of his kinsmen
he's oblivious,
content to turn
upon his nephew

for a meal.
Both the proposition
and the proof
of his black thesis,

he distinguishes
his every roost
like a venerable
family Bible.

Caged Crow

For exercise, he stretches
his wings to their limits
and flaps them wildly
several times each day.
His keeper found him
lifeless on the ground,
stunned unconscious
by a too close bolt
of lightning, wrapped him
in a black towel,
and laid him in the bottom
of a vacant parrot cage.
When Crow came to,
he blinked, rose shakily
to his feet, and in due time
scaled the cage mesh
to the perch. Weeks later,
fat with natural food,
he watched his keeper
open the cage door
and back slowly away.
Crow never even
tried to leave, satisfied
with his daily exercise,
exultant in his blue-
black heaven of stench,
caw, lore and sheen.

Old Crow

He gazes at the world
through the scratched, milky lens
of his good eye, his bad eye
punctured in his youth

by a rival floundering
in its death throes.
The eldest of his kind
in the wilderness,

he never ventures
far from his perch
in a centenarian oak,
cawing now and then,

content to rattle
against the shell of odds
his tasty kernel
of longevity.

He relishes
the daily indigestion
rumbling in the caldron
of his bowels,

each burp and act
of flatulence
stinking up his roost
with the strange perfume

of his milestone
so rarefied
it'd make the dreaded
stench of death a blessing.

He's the Dark Mercury

sluicing
through the hourglass
of our niggardly,
allotted time.
His caw
wobbles planets,

grinding
on their axes
toward oblivion.
He steels our hackles,
jagging down the stave
of our ennui

with the thunderbolt
of fable.
Our nostrils
flare, tearing
from the fumes
of his bile

beseeching
the quill
to scrawl
the abstruse
history
of the shadow.

Crows in the Rain

In a deluge
at midnight, backlit
by thunderbolts,
they loom
like remnants

of black
umbrellas,
ribs snapped,
turned inside out
by windblast, crammed

into the crotches
of a pine,
their ostensible
surrender
to the storm

belied
by the integrity
of fabric
impervious to wind
and water,

woven
by a goddess
scoffing at nylon,
opting for fibers
of blue-black iron.

Unabridged

Their only god
is sated bowels,
their only evil
the quest for their next
meal. Each of them
is a genius

with a perfect IQ
of instinct.
Their caw
is a dictionary,
unabridged,
blackened with the ink

of a letterless
alphabet.
They even
eat their children,
sparing a few
now and then

not for love but ink,
to scrawl because they must,
on the parchment
of oblivion,
the bold, black line
of their blood.

The Pure, White Crow

The moment she glimpsed his eggshell beak
and feet tinged with pink, his mother snatched him
from the rubble of his shell, and flung him

from her nest. He landed far below in a thatch
of pine needles, bruised but miraculously
alive. His finder fed him with an eyedropper,

nursed him to maturity, and sold him
to a circus. They kept him in a gilded cage,
and crowds came far and wide to see him.

He never knew the scourge of inclement weather,
and feasted on a smorgasbord fit for royals.
One daybreak, at the height of his prime

and stretching, he staggered, fell from his perch,
shuddered in the fresh, deep snow of his plumes,
and died, leaden with his longing for blackness.

Were I a Crow

I'd wear the moonless night
like black, calfskin gloves
fitted snugly as a layer

of new skin. As satisfied
with carrion as a serving
of fresh, bloody flesh,

I would eat, regarding
my offspring as meat
put away in a freezer.

I'd lord the cobalt ether
of fable, rattling the cosmos
with the vulgar, guttural

baritone of my caws.
Nights, I'd roost in a crotch
of a huge, dead tree

with the nine other
inkblots of my murder,
a mite-infested Rorschach

revealing as we breathe
the ravenous, reeking
psyche of our kind.

from *Uncle Ernest*

The Worshipers

Late at night
he would steal away
from his bedroom
to that secret place
in the woods,
just to watch them.
His heart would shake
his whole chest
and his breath would jerk
like a trapped rat.
He would watch them
through the dark leaves
clasping black crosses
as their chants
rose and fell
in the warm glow
of black candles.
They would kneel
at their bleating,
black animal
as hands Ernest knew
were not their own
grabbed candlelit knives
to quench the bloodlust
of their very
human ritual.

Stained Overalls

That early morning
in lined coats
and stained overalls
in January
well below freezing
when Ernest stood
with the neighbors
at the site
of his first hog kill,
a big, red hog
of thick-slabbed bacon,
fat sausage patties,
that early morning
when the neighbor's sons
slugged it out
just over who
would slash the throat,
that early morning
when young boys trembled
ankle-deep in blood,
so much blood
Ernest was certain
the whole sunrise
had been gutted.

In His Dream

Dreaming wildly
of cherubs
Ernest sleeps
on his stomach
in his pitch black
asylum room.
Incipient lust
heats his loins
like an illness
and leaves his member
a heavy sponge,
sopped, pulsing
with his blood.
Ernest rolls over
on his side
and wakes smiling
at his lust,
at his thick fingers
smearing on the sheet
his warm, unconscious
ejaculate.

White Plastic Knives

Ernest hears
Agnes walking
down the bright white hall
for therapy.
Just yesterday
she sat with Ernest
at a picnic
for the patients.
Her doctor stopped by
with his paper plate
of overcooked meat
and bright white
plastic utensils,
her young doctor
whose knife kept breaking
on the hardened meat.
Agnes kept grinning.
Now she sits
in his white office
and fixes herself
for a session.
Ernest hears the crisp
hairline fracturing
of white plastic knives
and sees Agnes
grinning deep
beneath her dazzling,
thick carapace
of pathology.

Windowsill

The infirmary
where Ernest sits
to be sutured
is seething with light,
the garish light
of purest science.
He fixes his eyes
on the instruments
of physicians
and sees a cousin
whom he visited
as a child.
The cousin
was a wizard
of purest science
and Ernest still sees
his deft maneuver
of the scalpel
in the breasts of birds.
Ernest still sees
the row of jars
on the cousin's
windowsill,
the jars of hearts,
the perfect,
pickled hearts
of little sparrows.

Deep Blues

a Sunday morning
in April
and a chapel
under heavy guard
where Ernest opens
his dark wine hymnal,
moves his lips,
but can't sing.
He closes his eyes
and sees deep blues
the hues of bruises
from a beating
for playing with kids,
young black kids.
He sees himself
hunkering
in a leafy shade
near the country
Baptist church
and he hears again
the hundred
black voices
rapt in song,
the spirit
that moved them
creeping through the woods
like early spring.

Blue Moon

This night's late,
thick as black syrup,
and tomorrow's
the first day
of Ernest's furlough.
His mother tries
but simply can't sleep
watching a full moon
bleed into her room
and cast black shadows
at her bed's edge.
It's that feeling
almost sexual
breaking on her brow
in cold sweat,
that feeling
of pure, simple love,
that motherly
violent love
piqued with stark terror.
She snuggles her head
in her pillow's down
but simply can't sleep
for her dark
cheekbone probing
of brand-new,
cold blue steel.

The Faded Snapshot

Ernest's mother
hears him snoring
in the back bedroom.
In the clabbered dark
of her own home
she clenches both fists
at the thought
of her bastard ex
who left her
eight months pregnant
with Ernest
and his twin sister.
She turns on her lamp
and studies
the faded snapshot
of Ernest
with his dead sister
and sees her ex
in the sister's face
and her very self
as a child
in Ernest's.
The lamp turned off
she sleeps again
to the cadence
of Ernest's breathing.
She sleeps again
with the chilling,
secret favor
her favored child
did his dear mother,
but must never know.

Warm Eggs

On the third day
of his furlough
Uncle Ernest
squats in the hen house
in the shadows
of first light.
He reaches
for a pair
of warm eggs
and sees the buttocks
of his infant niece.
His dead sister screams
as he strokes
the warm eggs.
He never meant
to harm the child
but just to rub
the plump buttocks
in the shadows
of a world
where love, lust, and touch
were features
of the same egg.
He never meant
to hack to death
his sis who saw him
and kept screaming.
Uncle Ernest
grips the eggs
in his huge right hand
and heads home.

The Folding Wings

In fathoms
of asylum calm
Ernest stirs awake,
yawning at midnight.
His eyes catch
what light there is,
swathe it with warm lids,
and let it dance
in white galleries
of consciousness.
He sees himself stooped
with a hose
of running water
flooding the birdbaths
and blooming gardens
of his brain
and he yawns again
in his dark,
little room, its walls
the folding wings
of owls, dreaming.

from *The Lobsterman's Dream: Poems of the Coast of Maine*

The Ocean

Even when it's calm,
the locals hear
its nearby roar
at the shoreline.

Almost imperceptibly,
to its constant drumbeat,
the wavy window panes
of old cottages

rattle in their frames.
The locals
rasp their salt-
encrusted names.

It looms
just over the gentle
granite rise
like, flat on a table,

a dark,
forbidding book
braced for yet another
fracturing of its spine.

Monhegan Island

The shipwrecks,
say the locals,
off its windward side
number in the hundreds,

its windward side
where the ocean
drops immediately
to a depth

of hundreds of feet
beneath its cliffs
of steep,
solid granite

rising to a height
of one hundred sixty feet,
both the steepest
and the highest

of the Maine seaboard.
The mammoth sea swells
battering the granite
are spectacular,

ideal
for the lurid,
whether sightseer
or suicide.

Dory

Even beached, it reeks
of the deep Atlantic.
Resting on the rocky shore
but feet above the dark

demarcation of high tide,
it basks in sea-like hues
of blackish green and blue.
Its bottom is flat

for ballast, wide planks
fastened lengthwise
from bow to stern,
never steam bent,

sawn to the natural
curve defining its shape.
Its prow is high
and proud; its stern

the solemn "tombstone."
It basks in the sun:
ominously green and blue;
at home in any weather;

deceptively strong;
and sans a whit of frill,
exactly what the sea,
if wood, would be.

Scrimshaw

Intricate schooners
carved on whalebone
dangle from her wrinkled,

elongated earlobes.
She hasn't spoken
since the day she learned,

fifty years ago,
she'd lost her only son
to the briny darkness

of Davy Jones's locker,
her grief frozen
on the verge of breaking,

unforgiving as,
fixed and shattering
with hairline cracks

on the dark
canvas behind her,
the crests of Homer's oil*.

*The Fog Warning (oil on canvas by Winslow Homer)

The Warning

(painting by Jamie Wyeth, 2007)

Deep hues
of blue, black and green
vie for preeminence
in the swells.

The Atlantic has succumbed
to the fathomless,
implacable issues
of its anger.

The gull's feet
dangle beneath its breast
like gaunt rag dolls,
the gull

staring down the viewer
head-on, as if
any minute now
it will soar from the canvas

and plaster its body
against the glass,
the imaginary glass
shielding the viewer

from the fierce, black hells
of its eyes.

The Lobster

Its exoskeleton's graced
with the greenish-black hue
of the Atlantic
on whose shadowy bed

it's eked out a life
of five decades.
Its crusher claw
could snap off the thumb

of a lobsterman.
Through touch, taste,
and smell, it has mastered
its hostile habitat.

Tonight, electric
with the scent
of rancid bait,
it will struggle

through the netted tunnel
of a trap,
tear asunder
the flesh of its frantic

sister, and it will feast,
rapacious as the socialite
of Cape Cod, who,
by late tomorrow evening,

in the candlelit ambiance
of The Lobster Pot,
will sink her gleaming teeth
into its meat.

The Lobsterman's Dream

He's been out since first light
running his traps. The temperature
is falling, and black-green ice
starts building at the bow of his boat.

The blows of his sledgehammer
just chip its edges as if he were
an Indian tediously chipping flint
into an arrowhead. Breathing heavily,

he keeps taking the sledge to the ice,
the black-green ice thickening, pulling
his boat downward, as if the sea,
relentless in its cold, briny resolve,

were stiffening and dwindling him
to a hapless figure frozen for the ages,
tumbling through the leagues of the black-
green glass of a paperweight.

The Lighthouse Keepers

For each working year of their lives,
a man and his wife were the keepers.
They relished the isolation,
oaring begrudgingly to the mainland

once a month for books, music and food.
Their music was classical,
their sea deliciously avant-garde.
During what leisure the light allowed,

they detonated their doldrums
with the pliant little bombs of their books.
They spoke but to see if they still could.
One November day, when they were old,

they left for no one knew where,
the light they kept all those years
enough, almost, for the fogged,
inexorable coming of the night.

Mainers

For the Atlantic,
for hundreds of years,
they've penned

and sung their hymns.
Its bounty
feeds their young,

fattening them out
for prosperity
or icy blue slaughter.

Even their eyes
are hued
with its blues

and blackish greens,
this hallowed brine
which, in the same breath

it nurtures them,
lobs the flowered wreaths
for their dead.

Tide Pool Touch Tank

(for Frank)

The dank air
of the Maine State Aquarium
is pungent with brine
and the nostril-flaring
smell of fresh fish.

Little children huddle
around a tank
like primitives in a ritual.
Their heads swim
with flashbacks

of moonless, blue-black skies,
of luminous bodies
sparkling through the slats
of their cribs
beside the windows,

ever beyond the reach
of their fat, groping fingers.
Wide-eyed, entranced
by the miracle beneath them,
they take deep breaths,

ease their hands into the black-
green holiness of seawater,
and, with the fingers of gods
trembling in the heavens,
stroke the spiny skin of stars.

from Chapbooks:

The Circus

Plain Pine

Five Lavender Minutes of an Afternoon

The Red, Candlelit Darkness (complete)

The House of Mirrors

(from The Circus*)*

Its vertical surfaces
are concave, convex and wavy,
painted with a smooth film of silver
so pure it's scarcely there.
Its aisles are laid out in a maze.
Its mirrors, the Beatitudes
objectified, are ever giving back
all that they receive.
Having been brought face-to-face
with each monstrous masking
of their guile, the visitors
emerge from it terrified
ad nauseam, baptized
in the horror of their selves.

The Clown

(from The Circus*)*

practices his silly acts
in the circus of minutes.
Rainbows snake, kink, and frizzle
from his scalp. It takes him hours

to paint his torturous face,
just to get it sad enough.
Mime is the art that sparkles
in the night show of his life.

His friends are siamese twins,
his bastard child a human
cannonball. For wise counsel,
he eavesdrops the dreams of freaks.

Juggling is his calculus,
slapstick his highest physics.
On the straw of beasts he sleeps.
His mute soul rings with laughter.

The Elephant Man

(from The Circus*)*

(after The Elephant Man*, a David Lynch Film)*

Torchlight, like the yolk of a cracked egg,
trickles down the pockmarked, massive
folds of flesh clinging to a skull
and glints straw stuck in the hair

of a bulbous ear. Breath rattles like air
forced from the folds of ragged bellows.
He spends his days on display
to the gasps and stares of passersby.

Nights, during moments of privacy
allotted him in the squalor of his tent,
he fashions bits of straw into miniature bricks,
and with his mortar of homemade glue,

at the painstaking rate of an inch a year,
raises the walls and spires of his cathedral,
magnificent almost as the mute,
ravishing beauty of his dream.

The Fat Lady

(from The Circus*)*

Fine wine and gourmet repasts
fill her ravenous soul like sunlight

sucked through the stained-glass straws
of a sanctuary.

Her mouth enshrines the warm,
sophisticated muscle of her tongue.

The perfect notes of arias
leap from the sheen of her painted lips.

She moves with the fluid grace of waves
lapping the bountiful shores of her presence,

her corpulence a rare white oyster
swaddling the pearl of her dainty skeleton.

Fathoms of lavender silk
straddle her fabulous girth.

Hermaphrodite

(from The Circus*)*

He feels the world with her
skin and nerves; love, the allure
of an insoluble puzzle.
It must suffice, the it of a thing
inanimate, finding,
because it must, beauty
in the curse and the monster;
feeling the rush of the same blood
to the genitals of a budding man
and woman, fashioned of the same
ounces of warm flesh
pulsing in the loins of a freshly
pubescent child, wild with wonder.

Siamese Twins

(from The Circus*)*

The darkness is the archive
of their loss where the stars,
grinding to their billions-
of-years-long halts, spin

for a while, spit-shining
their patent leather shoes.
The colorblind philosopher
amuses herself with her Rubik's

Cube of logic, a tone-deaf
organ grinder hard on the heels
of her dark, arbitrary monkey,
while the poet, her brooding twin

with perfect pitch, croons
the dictionary-thick oeuvre
she knows just might, with luck,
get them through the night.

Cool Water

(from Plain Pine*)*

The bedclothes
damp with the sweat
of human sickness,
Pauline wrenches her body
in troubled dream-sleep.
Even the moonglow
is nothing but frost
where the pines
with their bark
of glazed ice
keep creaking
in the night.
Amos hears them
through the shack walls
and he hears
the labored breathing
of his wife
delirious
with high fever.
She wakes refusing
his raspy offer
of a sip
of cool water,
licks the slight bleeding
of heat-split lips,
and braces her delirium
for his mount.

The Dark Child

(from Plain Pine*)*

Their shack hunkers
deep, deep in the woods
and its tin roof creaks
with the coming cold.
Her long, loosened braids
are oiled with the bronze
of her body ooze.
She jerks in her nightmare
with her back next to his,
his overalls crumpled
in the chair beside him,
stinking, stiffening
with the blood of wild doves.
Their fire dies as they sink
deeper and deeper into sleep,
the black night scooting in close
like a dark, whimpering child.

Plain Pine

(from Plain Pine*)*

As Pauline sleeps
in the dawn-glow,
Amos studies
her unfinished pair
of miniature buzzards.
He can't help
but notice
how their perfect heads
stretch skyward
on thin, naked necks
and their half-
whittled wings
struggle violently
in the knots
of plain pine
like the straining
arms of men
freeing themselves
from a pit
of quicksand,
these tiny
wooden buzzards
already putrid
with the dark
gift of life
his very wife
is giving them.

The Big Red Rooster

(from Plain Pine*)*

was a gift to Amos
from his brother.
Pauline was home alone
late that night
and she still sees
her bedroom light
raging in an eye
pupilled with the bead
of her rifle.
She still sees
the big red rooster
thrashing on its back
and its grand wings
staked to the earth
with black paws,
and she still feels
her right index finger
freezing at the trigger
and herself
just standing there
and watching
as the one-eyed skunk
closed in for the kill.

Her Untowelled Woods

(from Plain Pine*)*

are still drenched
from a shower
of wild rain.
Pauline walks barefoot
to the spot
where lightning
just hours before
struck her tallest pine
and burned it
to the black earth.
She squats
near the stump
whose fat
scabby roots
are the feet
of a huge crow
the last of its kind
still hunkering
ever closer
to the black earth,
still smoldering,
still mustering up
its final
bloodcurdling caw.

"Mama Sug"

(from Five Lavender Minutes of an Afternoon*)*

(in memory of Margaret Ann Elizabeth Coleman)

Of blocks of native Texas limestone,
the house they kept on their slim pension
was built in the 1800's.
Summer afternoons, unpretentious
as the dough each morning at first light

she'd pummel with her fists into biscuits,
she'd waddle her weary corpulence
to the rocker on her wooden porch,
her slat bonnet tied in a bow
snug against the flab of her throat.

For her own burial, so as not
to burden her children or grandchildren,
she kept what little cash she'd saved
rolled in a cotton pouch and safety-
pinned to what was left of her bra.

Although ever clad in a long cotton dress
and brown cotton hose she rolled down
the tops of just below her knees,
she never wore corsets or underdrawers,
prudently comforting her womanhood

ravaged by conjugal obligations
and the savage natural births
of ten children. Even the snuff
she'd pack into her labial vestibule
with a flat wooden spoon, was Honest.

Five Lavender Minutes of an Afternoon

(from Five Lavender Minutes of an Afternoon*)*

Mother Worrell, Dad's paternal grandmother,
was the sledge which drove the spike of religion
deep into the huge, virgin heart of Mama.

From then on, for the better part of five decades,
Mama felt she never measured up to the Beatitudes.
Despite her fervor in attending church services

at least three times per week and her diligence
in keeping the house alien to cigarettes or a single
can of beer, she wallowed in the mire of shame,

save five minutes of the afternoon following
another day of grammar school when Bobo and I
walked into the den and found her reclining

sideways on the sofa, her head propped up by her arm.
Her hair freshly coiffed, her body clad in a stylish
lavender evening gown ending at her heels,

she greeted us with forced sophistication, inquiring
how our day had gone. As she spoke, she took, deep
into her lungs, drags off a long, filtered Lucky Strike,

exhaling smoke rings wobbling like halos
above her fine coiffure before unraveling in the air.
Too shocked to speak, we watched her act as if nothing

were unusual, taking deep drags, exhaling.
After a few minutes, she sat up on the sofa, crunched
the cigarette into a brand-new lavender ashtray,

laughed, and said she was just kidding. As she laughed,
the last of her smoke rings hovered for a moment
above her head and vanished, fleeting as her stint in sin.

Baby Horny Frogs (Texas Horned Lizards)

(from Five Lavender Minutes of an Afternoon*)*

We'd stand them on dimes,
turn them on their backs,
and coax them asleep
stroking their bellies
gently with the tips

of our forefingers.
Kay's finger was long
and slender, its nail
bright with red polish.
I'll never forget

the day she asked me
to lie on my back
on red sand beneath
the stand of mesquites
just outside the view

of my vigilant
mother, watching us
intermittently
through the small window
above her kitchen

sink. I swear it burned,
that edge of Kay's nail,
circling my navel,
stirring my blood toward
anything but sleep.

Lake Balmorhea (far West Texas)

(from Five Lavender Minutes of an Afternoon*)*

As we rowed out
to the middle of the lake to fish,
we'd watch Mama growing smaller,
sitting on a rock at the lake's edge.

She'd sit for hours,
staring at the distant Davis Mountains,
her gaze intent as a playwright's
fixed on the first performance

of her masterpiece,
a complex play which,
because she penned it,
only she understood,

each mountain a character
miraculous in the blue
of development, ravishing
in the changing, desert light.

The Red, Candlelit Darkness

(Chisos Mining Company, Early 1900s, Terlingua, Texas)

I. Silver Pesos

Candy and Blue Denim

Though Juan had watched
Diego, his older cousin,
die in a dark cloud
of tremors and confusion,
he kept remembering
what Diego said
he liked about his life
in Terlingua: shopping
at the Chisos Store
with wages double
what miners made in Mexico.
Diego smiled as he talked
about the silver pesos
cradled in his palm
even when his fingers reddened:
about the bright hard candy
and blue, unblemished denim
bagged by the smiling clerk.

The Warning

Just before sunrise,
Juan is jogging
toward the Rio Grande
to take a coveted job

with the Chisos Mining Company.
When the curandero appears,
as if from nowhere,
to warn him of the perils
of the mine, Juan never flinches,
saying he fears neither blood
nor death. As the old man rasps,
Juan remembers the soiled
and tattered Mexican
history book he studied
in school: how its pages
reeked of the iron-rich
smell of blood. Juan remembers
how all its chilling stories
ended in death, dark
and ubiquitous as the shadows
in sunlight. Juan never flinches,
saying he fears neither the iron-
rich blood nor the death
ubiquitous as the shadows.

Little Rivers

In his dream, the silver crosses
chained to the necks of virgins
are melting, sizzling down the cleavage
of their breasts, searing the flesh
of abdomens, thighs, legs and feet,
rushing in little rivers
toward the Rio Grande.
In his dream, the silver crucifixes
hanging on the sanctuary walls
are melting, leaving trails of fire
on the stone cathedral walls
and ancient wooden floors,

rushing beneath the doors in little rivers
toward the Rio Grande.
The crosses and the crucifixes
are melting, scorching the muddy bottom
of the Rio Grande, rushing
up the banks on the Texas side
and brimming the flasks
gleaming near the mouth
of the growling Chisos mine.

The Bruja

The devils flesh her bones
with clumps of cinnabar.
In dreams, she comes to him,
and they stand face to face,
each inches from the other's
wide-eyed stare. Her breath
reeks of the deep, red earth,
and she has no eyelids.
Spells writhe in her palms
like baby diamondbacks
for which he reaches
but never touches.
Her beady eyes are quick
with hot, wobbling silver.

II. Rawhide Buckets

The Miracle

He labors all day
deep in the red,

candlelit darkness
of the mine, musing
the five o'clock
miracle sure to come
when his wages
of Mexican silver pesos
will turn, right
before his eyes,
into water fit
for drinking, dried
corn tortillas, beans,
dried chili for seasoning,
a little candy, and even
a shaving or two of cheese.

The Faces

of cinnabar
loom deep
within the thick,
palpable darkness
of the desert:
faces the miners
take their picks to:
faces feebly lit
by little candles
fastened to their hats:
faces crumbled
to fill wagons
for droplets of quick-
silver: wagons
the burros,
staggering, groaning,
and bleeding,
drag in sunlight.

Like the Hands of Bronze-fleshed Clocks

With notched poles and sure,
nimble feet, they descend
the velvety darkness
of the mine shaft,
fill the rawhide buckets
with cinnabar, and strap them
to their backs. With notched
poles and sure, nimble feet,
loaded with buckets
of cinnabar, they ascend
the velvety darkness
to the hot, glaring mouth
of the mine, and dump
their cargo into the carts
only to descend again;
descending, ascending
again and again like the hands
of bronze-fleshed clocks
measuring and recording
the brutal, interminable
hours of their days.

The Burning

Fearing a breach of either
could cost him his job,
Juan honors
his unspoken vows
of secrecy and loyalty
to the Chisos Store.
Hence, he strikes the friend
who whispers, handing him
the mail-order catalog.

The coals of the fire
for his cabrito
are still smoldering.
Watchfully and quietly,
he tears the pages
from the catalog spine,
wads them into balls,
and burns them.
The flames they make
cast terrible shadows
on the adobe walls,
the shifting shadows
of things forbidden,
dark and unforgiving
as cardinal sin.

III. The Dazzling Burro

The Mouths

Every morning,
heading to the mouth
of the mine,
they study
their fingers
for the slightest hint
of the redness
they fear will come:
the redness, tremors,
loosening
of their teeth,
bleeding gums,
and frothing
at the mouth

they fear will come,
steal their jobs,
and send them
back to Mexico
and long, dark nights
clotted with dreams
of wages
they once made
for food and clean,
new clothing.

Red

the cinnabar
crumbled
by his pick;
red his nose,
cheeks,
and fingers;
red the bloodstains
on his pillow,
the faint
bloodstains
the only
roses
he'll ever know.

The Sounds of Devils

From the depths of hell itself,
in the suffocating glare
of the afternoon, the burros
pull the wobbling carts
of cinnabar. With but half

of their workday behind them,
drenched with sweat,
they shine like dark,
faceted crystal twisted
in the sun. Every night
for weeks, after *retiring*
as a miner, too sick to work
and dying in the cool adobe
house of his aunt in Mexico,
he'll wake burning with fever
and sweating from his fitful sleep
to the sounds of devils
belting out the arias
of hell: the sounds
the dazzling burro makes
dying in the bright Texas sun.

The Screams

Every winter,
on cold, moonless nights
at the cemetery,
I hear them
whooshing like ghosts
trapped in a bell jar,
some from the joy
of a job, others
bubbling with blood
and the frothy spit
of a rabid dog.
Every winter,
on cold, moonless nights
at the cemetery,
so muffled
they're barely audible,

they swish
inside the snifters
of my ears
like scorpions
issuing from the buried,
each dark grave
the caved-in shaft
of a small Chisos mine.

About the Author

In 1998, Larry D. Thomas retired from a career in social service and adult criminal justice, and has since that time devoted full time to his poetry. Prior to his retirement in 1998 as a branch director of the Harris County Adult Probation Department, he maintained a disciplined practice of writing poems on weekends for over twenty years, and was successful in publishing his work in numerous respected national literary journals, to many of which he earned the distinction of being a regular contributor. Among the journals his poems appeared in were the *Southwest Review, Poet Lore, The Cape Rock, The Small Pond Magazine of Literature, The Chattahoochee Review, Writers' Forum, Louisiana Literature, Puerto del Sol, The Texas Review, Borderlands: Texas Poetry Review,* and *Southwestern American Literature.*

Timberline Press (Fulton, MO) brought out his first collection of poetry in 2001, a chapbook titled *The Lighthouse Keeper,* published in handset letterpress with original linocut illustrations. The volume was selected by the *Small Press Review* as a "Pick of the Month," and quickly sold out two printings. His first book-length collection of poetry, *Amazing Grace,* was published by *Texas Review* Press in 2001 as winner of the *Texas Review* Poetry Prize. The collection also won the Western Heritage Wrangler Award, sponsored by the National Cowboy & Western Heritage Museum in Oklahoma City, OK, one of the top national awards granted annually to a collection of poetry which celebrates the historical or contemporary American West. He has published eight additional full-length collections of poems, several of which have received distinguished prizes and awards. *Where Skulls Speak*

Wind, published by *Texas Review* Press in 2004, received both the 2004 *Texas Review* Poetry Prize and the 2004 Violet Crown Book Award (Writers' League of Texas), one of the top literary awards in Texas granted annually for a book-length collection of poetry. Among the many additional honors and awards he has received for his poetry are a 2007 Poets' Prize nomination for *Stark Beauty* (West Chester University/Nicholas Roerich Museum); six Pushcart Prize nominations; a Best of the Net nomination; seven Spur Award Finalist citations from Western Writers of America, and the 2015 Western Heritage Wrangler Award (National Cowboy & Western Heritage Museum). The Texas Legislature, in April, 2007, appointed Mr. Thomas as the 2008 Texas Poet Laureate. In April, 2009, he was inducted into the Texas Institute of Letters. Thomas has published over five hundred poems in distinguished journals throughout the United States and in China, Mexico, Ireland and Australia.

Although Thomas was born and raised in West Texas, he moved to Houston at the age of twenty, and resided there from 1967 until 2011. In April, 2011, he and his wife, Lisa, moved to Alpine in far West Texas where they currently reside.

Thomas's first three book-length collections of poems were resonant with a strong sense of place, from West Texas where he was born and reared to southeast Texas and the Gulf Coast where he lived his entire adult life until the age of sixty-four when he moved back to West Texas. The subjects of his subsequent poetry collections are intriguingly diverse, including outlaw bikers, ekphrasis, the avian world, an asylum for the criminally insane, and the coast of Maine.